Paper

Claire Llewellyn

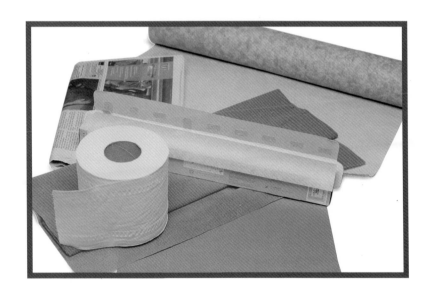

SEA-TO-SEA

Mankato Collingwood London

This edition first published in 2006 by
Sea-to-Sea Publications
1980 Lookout Drive
North Mankato
Minnesota 56003

Printed in China

Library of Congress Cataloging-in-Publication Data

Llewellyn, Claire.
  Paper/by Claire Llewellyn
    p. cm. — (I know that!)
  ISBN 1-932889-54-X
  1. Paper—Juvenile literature. 2. Papermaking—Juvenile literature. I. Title.

TS1105.5.L58 2005
676—dc22

                                    2004063716

9 8 7 6 5 4 3 2

Published by arrangement with the Watts Publishing Group Ltd, London

Series advisor: Gill Matthews, nonfiction literacy consultant and Inset trainer. Editor: Rachel Cooke. Series
design: Peter Scoulding. Designer: James Marks. Photography: Ray Moller unless otherwise credited.
Acknowledgments: Mark Edwards/Still Pictures: 17b. Hewlett Packard: 9t. Alan Majchrowicz/Still Pictures: 14.
Sally Morgan/Ecoscene: 16, 17t. Helene Rogers/Art Directors/Trip: 13b. Syracuse Newspapers/Image
Works/Topham: 19t. J.C. Vincent/Still Pictures: 15. Thanks to our models Jaydee Cozzi, Jakob Hawker,
Hayley Sapsford and Phoebus Zavros

Contents

Paper is useful

Paper is a very useful material.
It is used to make all sorts of things.

▼ *These things are all made of paper.*

Paper towels

Writing paper

Banknotes

Bag

Can you think of three other things that are made of paper?

Cup

Tissues

Plate

Magazine

Book

5

All kinds of paper

There are many kinds of paper.
Each one has its own look and feel.

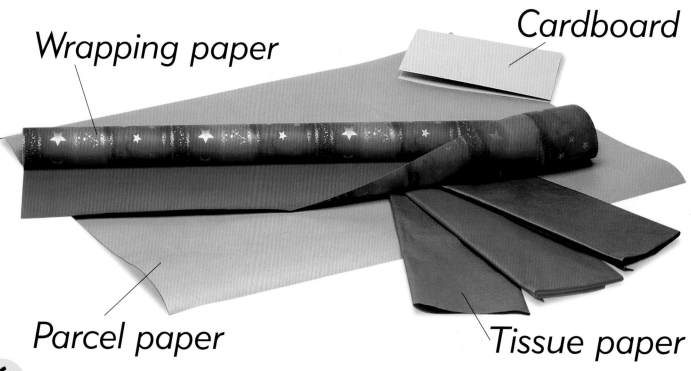

Wrapping paper

Cardboard

Parcel paper

Tissue paper

6

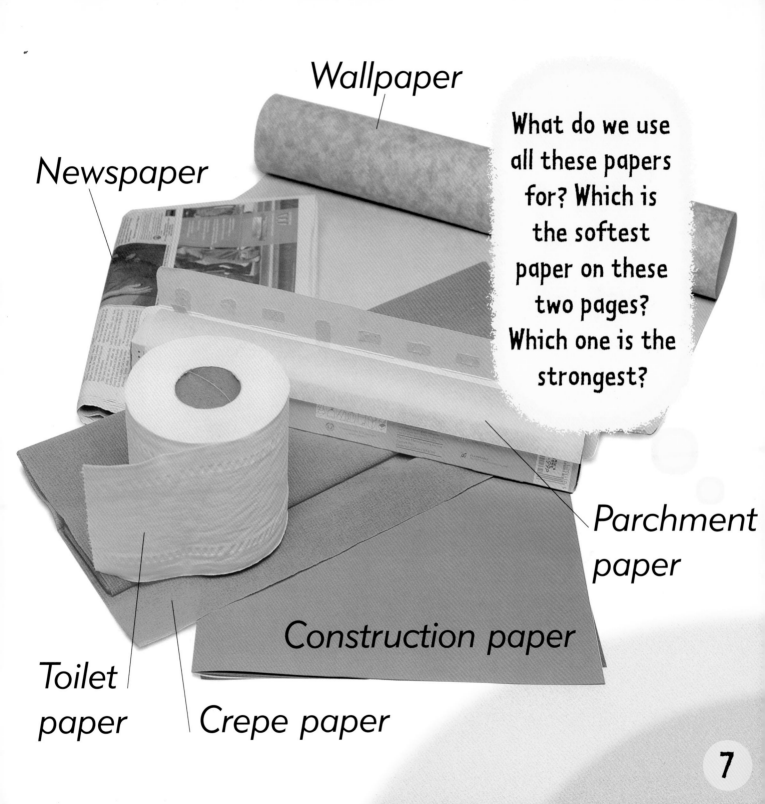

Wallpaper

Newspaper

What do we use all these papers for? Which is the softest paper on these two pages? Which one is the strongest?

Parchment paper

Construction paper

Toilet paper

Crepe paper

7

We write on paper

Paper is very smooth.

 Paper is easy to write on and paint on.

▶ *Machines can print on paper, too.*

We cannot write on all paper. What happens when you write on soft paper with a felt-tip pen?

Paper is strong

Some paper is very strong.
We use it to pack
and protect things.

▶ *Some foods
are packed
in paper.*

◀ *A strong cardboard box is always useful.*

Some things break very easily. Soft paper helps to protect them from bumps.

11

Paper soaks up water

Some paper is soft and
soaks up water.
We use it, then
throw it away.

▶ *We use paper
tissues to blow
our nose.*

We use paper towels to wipe up a spill.

Not all paper soaks up water. This paper cup and carton have been coated to make them waterproof.

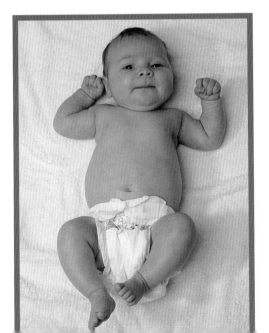

Paper diapers help to keep the baby dry!

13

Paper is made from wood

Paper is made from wood. Wood comes from trees.

Wood is a natural material. It is made by nature, not by people.

▲ *People grow trees for making paper in forests called plantations.*

▲ The trees are cut into logs and taken to a paper mill.

Making paper

At the paper mill, the logs are cut into bits. Then they are made into paper.

▶ *The bits of wood are mixed with water to make a soggy pulp.*

The pulp is spread into a long, flat sheet.

Sometimes old paper is used to make new paper. This is called recycling.

The sheet is flattened. It dries into paper.

How is the paper used?

Paper from the paper mill is used in different ways.

▶ *Some paper is cut into sheets.*

Look at a newspaper and this book. What is the same about the paper they are made of? What is different?

▲ *Some is used to make newspapers and books.*

◀ *Some goes to factories to make cardboard.*

Paper is easy to cut and shape

Paper is easy to work with.

▶ You can draw on it...

What things have you made out of paper?

fold it...

cut it...

curl it...

and stick it.

21

I know that...

1 Paper is useful.

2 There are many kinds of paper.

3 We write on paper.

22

4 Paper is strong.

5 Paper soaks up water.

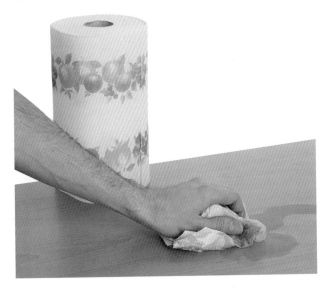

6 Paper is made from wood.

7 Paper is made at a paper mill.

8 The paper is cut up into sheets or used to make boxes, books, and newspapers.

9 Paper is easy to cut and shape.

Index

About this book

I Know That! is designed to introduce children to the process of gathering information and using reference books, one of the key skills needed to begin more formal learning at school. For this reason, each book's structure reflects the information books children will use later in their learning career—with key information in the main text and additional facts and ideas in the captions. The panels give an opportunity for further activities, ideas, or discussions. The contents page and index are helpful reference guides.

The language is carefully chosen to be accessible to children just beginning to read. Illustrations support the text but also give information in their own right; active consideration and discussion of images is another key referencing skill. The main aim of the series is to build confidence—showing children how much they already know and giving them the ability to gather new information for themselves. With this in mind, the *I know that...* section at the end of the book is a simple way for children to revisit what they already know as well as what they have learned from reading the book.